LATE STYLE

ADRIAN SILBERNAGEL

NANNY
GOAT
BOOKS

Nanny Goat Press
Louisville, KY

nannygoat.press

Late Style

First Edition.

ISBN: 978-1-954002-02-9

CONTENTS

"The late works are relegated to the outer reaches of art, in the vicinity of document. In fact, studies of the very late Beethoven seldom fail to make reference to biography and fate. It is as if, confronted by the dignity of human death, the theory of art were to divest itself of its rights and abdicate in favor of reality."

- Theodor Adorno

PREVIOUS APPEARANCES

Thank you to the following journals, in which selected poems from this work originally appeared:

Anthropocene
"Viva La Vida (Watermelons 1)" "Las Sandias (Watermelons 2)"

Drunk Monkeys
"Unfinished Painting"

The Indianapolis Review
"Self Portrait"

Invisible City
"The Answer Is No (First Attempt At Final Work)"

The Meadow
"Riding With Death / Yell An Eye For An Eye"

THE ANSWER IS NO (FIRST
ATTEMPT AT FINAL WORK)

AFTER KAY SAGE

We begin with the myth of potential,
end with a horizon
of blank canvases stretching into infinity.

I've done what was asked of me,
and lost interest in everything that boasts
a beginning and end, a discernible form.

Sometimes I close my eyes
and imagine a swarm of pastel suits
and pretty bonnets spilling over

green lawns, laughter overflowing
like champagne as my studio goes dark and I slip

into a private, perpetual Easter.
The opposite of beauty is not what people think,
even beautiful people

know an ugly duckling when they see one.
In the hunt for pleasure,
I'm a wild card, a candied razor,

a master eraser. I don't want them to find me,
but I do want them to try,
the way the mind tries

to fathom the vastness of oceans and stars
— hopelessly, ad infinitum.
If they find me, it's game over:

that's why I never put all of my eggs in one casket,
all my pills in one drawer.

YOUR MOVE (LAST ATTEMPT AT FINAL WORK)

AFTER KAY SAGE

This is how we make it up as we go along.
You plate the appetizers. I plate the desserts,
apologize to the guests when you storm off
mid-game.
You compromise your queen. I lose my king
and keep the piece. I swallow it, gag.
A book comes out, it bores you. You pawn it
and buy a new pool table. I decorate the pool balls
and hide them around the house like it's
Easter morning,
wait outside your tomb with my eyes closed
counting backward from infinity. You feel rushed.
I stop the clock. I feel cheated.
You ask what's wrong.
I don't answer. You guess and misfire. I darken
my aesthetic: replace my rooks with cartridges,
all empty but the one with my name on it.
You ask where your gun went. I drop hints
like immaculate eggs over a hot skillet.

I remember ghosts don't hunger.
I scrap the rules altogether.
Make breakfast for my last supper.

VIVA LA VIDA (WATERMELONS 1)

AFTER FRIDA KAHLO

I imagine you having a picnic
with one of your lovers.
The two of you laughing, a little drunk, looking up
just in time to see a streetcar careening toward you.
The driver overcorrects, saving your lives but badly
injuring several others. It isn't your fault, at least
not completely. People are messy, these triangles
we indulge in even messier. But what do you do?

I imagine you lifting the reddest slice
to your mouth, an explosion of pink mist,
juice dribbling down
your chin onto your white guayabera: once a
wedding shirt, now just casual attire.
I once thought true love
like true zest for life was rare,
I just didn't know how rare. I imagine you feeding
the bloody meat to her,
then to others. I've chosen carefully my colors.

LAS SANDIAS (WATERMELONS 2)

AFTER DIEGO RIVERA

Your pain was invisible
and then it was a mural
on a public building.
They say I caused it
but who are they to talk
to me about causes.
I gave my life to one.
I gave my love to many
who could not endure it.
You could endure anything:
any diagnosis, any bull
headedness, any betrayal.
They whisper *suicidio*
but I do not hear them.
I'm old and trying to work
summer fruit into a portrait
of my grief. A blackbird lands
on the watermelon
I brought to the cemetery

and stares at me, unmoving.
I won't begin until it leaves. Even
if the fruit spoils. Even
in death you are more loyal
to life than I'll ever be.

RELATED FORMS

AFTER JESSICA DISMORR

If my methods were juvenile, yours
were all blood, cum & conquer.

If I was camouflaged, you were camoufleur.
If muse-starved, I was scarcely in your favor.

If to be mirrored was your motive,
it was mutual; if to last forever, mutual.

If downtown there is still a muraled stairwell
that leads to two doors: one deadbolted, the other

boarded over—I got everything I asked for.
Despite delusions of grandeur. Despite the night

& day difference between underground
& sellout, invincible & adult.

If there was one thing I asked for,
it was not to be seen & not heard.

If I was dreadlocked or angst-filled,
moon-pale or ethereal, you were adamant:

I was doomed to unravel. If memory serves,
you said as much that night by the river

gone swollen with snowmelt, gone viral
from trying to level with the trestle, that night

when your camera caught my wandering
         eye & made
my mind derail: my string of conditionals cascading

graffiti & all into your stone-cold waters, your
         glass gaze,
your brick wall. If your light-hungry world turned

me rabid, turned me pixilated;
if "a picture speaks a thousand words"

is a truism another, keener poet already had
his way with—say *the apparition*

of these faces in the crowd, s ay *petals,*
on a wet, black bough—

there was nothing left to steal.

SELF PORTRAIT

AFTER ZORAN MUSIC

Bitter winter, precious little life
in sight. A house fly
crawls across a window
slick with frost. Pregnant

aroma of bergamot
and something burning
stirs up memories: orange trees,
a train suddenly breaking,

the landscape settling
like the surface of a lake
once the thing that you dropped
in it sinks. How I couldn't stop

mistaking the pale white hills
for heaps of bodies.
Like hundreds of glowing
sparks, they chased me

when I had to climb over them
to clear my way. A man's face bobs
in a bath of darkness.
What happened to it still happens

to the sun everyday.
Shining eyes begged me,
who could still walk, silently
for help. A cup of tea set out

on the table goes cold.
The fly circles the rim.
The stars close their eyes.
Day breaks.

SELF PORTRAIT FACING DEATH

AFTER PABLO PICASSO

I kicked the bucket & watched
the pure blue spasm
& paint the air:
the air pure blue

for a fraction of a second
& then clear again.
Let me be clear. I wasn't finished
with life: life was finished with me.

As I arrange my crayons
on her vanity, my blues
with my pinks, my greens
with my yellows,

the mirror asks where she went.
I answer like a child
cold-called in class:
with a look of pure terror.

RIDING WITH DEATH / YELL AN EYE FOR AN EYE

AFTER JEAN-MICHEL BASQUIAT

Death looks good
on horse skin
but better on buildings

I've been burning
through my rent money
riding a skeleton

from SoHo to the Bronx
and back again
I always come back

clean. They say progress,
I say same old shit
lower tolerance.

What kills me
is how the body forgets
how to breathe.

My new dealer's
cash only.
My old dealer declines

to comment on the lone
figure with devil horns
on his front door.

MAN ON A PARK BENCH

AFTER HORACE PIPPIN

You don't have to watch them
change color to gather
something's wrong here—

here is a tree that's going
through something deeply,
terminally internal. Who hasn't
been so sick and tired of this world
that it starts to show on his face,
his eyes sunken patches of earth

in some park where a squirrel's been
back to dig up the seeds
it buried for harsher conditions.

I'm from here, and can tell you
those conditions have come
and gone. Yet here I am
back at this bench,
like I forgot something
important here once.

MAN IN A CABBAGE FIELD

AFTER EDVARD MUNCH

This is what I know:
anything I see, taste, touch,
smell, grow is only here
because something else is here
no longer. The earth
and everything on it suffers
from a wasting disease. People can't live
on broth alone: they need flavor,
texture and color, meaning
the farmer needs the artist
as much as the reverse. If there was a god,
he'd be the terrible wind that cuts
through these fields, turning the cows
into perfect, frozen sculptures
as I spoon feed my sister
while my father recites dark scripture
in her Eleventh Hour. There are sounds
only certain species can hear,
frequencies so high it makes you wonder

if the earth itself is screaming. Belief
clings to the body
the way the scent of liquor clings to a crook
neck bottle. If the soul exists,
it has the ears of a wax moth, is filthy
like unwashed cabbage,
and its thirst is insatiable.

TREE ROOTS

AFTER VINCENT VAN GOGH

When I lost my first tooth, you told me of a window
of time in which the severed nerve
might still feel something.

This window, you said, was the reason
we had to be gentle with all living things
and once-living things.

This was after you discovered your pain
could be transferred into color
like sunlight into oxygen,

but before you forgot how
you, too, might still feel something.
I picture you struggling

to your feet like a flower
toward the sun, mechanically
clutching your brushes to your gun

19

-wound, then staggering home,
half-animal in your hunt for survival.
Now men in suits are saying *Wheatfield*

with Crows was your last work,
but I know this can't be true:
your last work was removed

from a windowless room:
a tangle of roots
loosed from the soil.

UNFINISHED PAINTING

AFTER KEITH HARING

A boy wakes up in the middle
of the night with nothing but the shirt on his back
and the crayon in his pocket. It's 1979.
There are no cell phones, no computers,
no VCRs, no cable.
Just the illusion of freedom,
raw talent, and time to kill.
He draws a purple subway like the ones
in the Big Apple
and gets settled. His first night
underground is a little lonely
so he draws some companions: purple crust punks,
purple Jesus Freaks,
purple drag queens.
He decorates the cold concrete walls
with purple dogs and flying saucers.
He draws a purple police officer
to keep him and his friends safe.
But when the officer sees his drawings on the walls,

he yells: "Hey kid! Those aren't your walls
to paint!"
So he draws a secret passage, and another,
and escapes. He gets lost
in the tunnels. He catches a sniffle. He draws
a doctor
who tells him about a virus that's causing
boys like him
to disappear. The boy
runs back to warn his friends,
but can't find them anywhere. He marches
bravely forward.
When his toes disappear he draws new toes. When
his nose disappears
he draws a new nose. When his crayon
gets worn down
to a little purple stub, he gasps: "I've
barely started my career!"
Frantically he sketches a canvas,
and makes a few purple marks
in the corner before the crayon slips
through his fingers.
He sobs: "Why did I just bring one crayon,
and not the whole box?"
But then the boy realizes the box would
run out, too,
and there would still be more things he
could have drawn.
The marvelous purple world washes over him.
He made it. It's enough.

BLACK ON DARK GREY

AFTER MARK ROTHKO

If the last time you went home had been a painting,
it would have been a Rothko: multiform,
untitled, black
on dark grey, executed just months before
the artist was found
bleeding out on his
kitchen floor with a blade in his hand.
You drove across the tundra like a wolf
in the debt of winter
looking for a courage like that. Fog
lifting from the trees
your father planted to shelter the crops
he hoped would feed
your family someday. A radio host quoting a
private letter in which the late Mother Teresa
confessed to not feeling
God's presence in her last half century. You felt
a shiver
of a memory of being swept clean by
something other, stronger, than your pain.

Outside your parents' house,
you watched a small boy struggle to
move a mountain of snow from the driveway
to the yard
before collapsing down next to his shovel,
looking up just in time to see
a murder of geese disappear behind a vast
white sheet.
You would not ask for anything again.

ÉTANT DONNÉS

AFTER MARCEL DUCHAMP

In a deep closet locked from within and lit
by a single gas lamp, I am building a bed of twigs
and a landscape with a waterfall

out of the materials you've been leaving
on my doorstep
for the last two decades: a lump of pigskin,
a bundle of sticks, a bolt of velvet.

My wartime rations, you called them.
For the last two decades you've been leaving me,
little by little, to my own devices:
a withered bouquet,

a shrinking wardrobe, a fistful of word-sand.
Piecemeal, I rescind my commitments
to the outside world. My bastard boxcar children

roam the streets of one hundred different cities,
shore up

in bottles on one hundred distant coasts
in one hundred strangers' poems. In deep shame

in the deep shade of a Saguaro, I am daydreaming
of hydroplaning, of a threshold, of a home
-wrecker's body. A black box cracks
open in the desert sun,

and from it spills a naked woman
you don't recognize,
even though you've met her hundreds of times,
her pale skin covered with petals

from the flowers you brought me,
the pine needles you picked
with your bare hands. I fall to your feet
and offer up my best explanation, my fattest lamb.

ZEBRA & PARACHUTE

AFTER CHRISTOPHER WOOD

A zebra appears on a rooftop terrace
of Villa Savoye near Paris. *Are you real
or am I dreaming?* Stranger than fiction
yet commoner, the truth is a meteor shower
hidden in plain sight. A dazzle of businessmen
returning from lunch in the city tipsy
swerve, blink, rub their eyes—
are strangers to the high
-speed collisions that occur
in our atmosphere. *Let me be straight
with you. I wasn't always this paranoid.
I've kissed boys on dark balconies
that girls wouldn't kiss in broad daylight.*
Picasso says the purpose of art
is to wash from the soul the dust
of daily life. I say it's to burn out
one's own impurities, to make scarce
whatever scares you, or doesn't
scare you enough. I'm so afraid I'll jump
from this ledge and fall into a field

of poppies, and keep falling.
I've painted myself into a corner
of sky, so I must go now
and dangle there, suspended
forever in time. But first I must add
a patch of shade, for your mother
and a parachute, for mine.

IT'S ALL ABOUT ME, NOT YOU

AFTER GREER LANKTON

Girls, say hello to our guest.
I didn't tell them you were coming
until yesterday after morning
face lifts. Apologies for the mess—
we've had a comorbidity
of issues. First the roof,
then the faucet, then Alice
started using again, and I can't
get Ana to touch her miniature
sandwich. Don't let them fool you:
all of my girls are perfect
opposites: Alice a landslide,
Ana more a weathering,
they all get their way
eventually. Alice, please
pour the curator some tea.
Now what kind of time frame
were you thinking? Molecular?
Geological? Imagine the damage
we'd do on a geological time scale.

You can't. So perhaps a civilization
or its aftermath. Heaps of clothes
and doll parts. A studio apartment
that appears to have been hit
by a tornado, or by the practiced
decline of the will. In hindsight
it will all look the same.
Just like my girls.

RYGEFANTOM

AFTER OVARTACI

Nature puts no colours wrongly side by side.
It's people who assign the wrong labels
to things and people who paint
such hideous, terrifying paintings.

And it hurts to be separated
when in love, and it hurts to be coupled
with something ugly and disgusting.

Some call me insane, some call me a man
but I've never had trouble making
friends from the wrappers and bits of bark
I gathered when I was a bird / I was happy

and when I was a bowl I was happy
and when I tell them my body
is a pipe my spirit travels through
they ask what I am smoking.

So I bite my tongue until it bleeds
orange and pink and whittle
my soul until there's a hole
where my pain used to be.

LIFE? OR THEATER?

AFTER CHARLOTTE SALOMON

A mouse and her mother leap to their deaths
to escape a predator. Granddaughter
watches intoxicated as a hawk swoops down
and carries off the snake in its talons.

When I say I'd rather spend 40 nights on the floor
of a crowded train than one more night
alone with him,
no one understands me—
except his other victims' ghosts.

Which animal am I? The perverse one that lives
and takes pleasure in another creature's suffering?
What counts as living? A little theaterics,

a little recklessness and a secret ingredient:
a killer is a riddle. When we get home
I make him breakfast for supper: three eggs,

a sprinkle of cheese, a secret ingredient.
As he eats, I paint him, and when he stops
gasping for air, I paint the door frame

so death's angel will pass over me.

THIS IS THE FLOODING OF SOCK RIVER

AFTER JOSEPH YOAKUM

When heaven's windows burst open
the rain fell and the river grew
like a snake belly after it's eaten
a whole coyote. That snake bit me good
but I sucked out the venom, got on
a raft and floated through Missouri
across the rainbow bridge
following the railroad
across the cobalt mountains
where the heart swells and the trees all smile
past the weeping pebble down
through the green valley
around the great silver falls
never mixing my colors
just laying them side by side
so that each of them could sing,
never stopping to name anything,
never carrying anything too heavy
with me, just these pencils and this
one fluid motion I'm mastering.

IN SEARCH OF THE MIRACULOUS

AFTER BAS JAN ADER

I'm not ready—this is only part two
of the triptych—my craft still begs for the sea
the way the passengers aboard the
Titanic once begged
to be extinguished—think bystander effect
of cosmic proportions—
God do these waves shimmer as they
prepare to devour me I say a prayer
for all I'm about to leave unfinished—my marriage
was still in its first layers when I kissed my wife
goodbye she said I tasted like salt—and
what is prayer if not a lazy apology
asking forgiveness
when you should have asked permission—
like how you did when you left my father
bleeding out on the forest floor—teaching me
intention is immaterial—that no matter
how good you are
or how much human potential you harbor
you'll be tormented in this life and in the next

you'll be deciduous—stationery, love-starved—
maybe still capable of becoming something
utilitarian—a small sailboat or an acoustic guitar—
one man's death is another man's artwork like
one man's dad is another man's martyr—
if we make it back to shore I hope we'll come back
humble barn animals—not the clairvoyant kind—
the kind running in circles stumbling slantward
as the world comes unhinged—I already know
it won't be easy—nothing artful ever is—

IN GRATITUDE

Thank you to Hallie Ruth Decke r, Elæ Moss, Margaret Rhee, Ivy Johnson, Orchid Tierney, M.J. Gette, Daniel Reetz, Delilah Kyle Hack, Jon Tenholder, Marya Hornbacher, Georgia Lacy, Jon Thrower, Jaime Jensen, Justine Egner, and others, for your editorial guidance and tireless encouragement + readership.

Thank you to all of the marginalized artists, without whose resistance and resilience this work would not be possible.

Thank you to Sarah Gardiner and Nanny Goat Press for taking a chance on us.

ABOUT THE AUTHOR

Adrian Silbernagel (he/him/his) is a writer, educator, and activist who lives in Louisville, KY.. His first book of poetry, *Transitional Object*, was published through the Operating System. He is the author of Thinking Queerly, a column at Queer Kentucky, and curator of Field Notes, a web series on creative practice/process at The Operating System. Adrian also facilitates inclusivity workshops through QueerKentucky.

www.ingramcontent.com/pod-product-compliance
Lightning Source LLC
LaVergne TN
LVHW051430080426
835508LV00022B/3335